Behind the Scenes with SAMMY

By Jena Doolas and Peter Kitzhöfer

CelebrationPress
An Imprint of ScottForesman

Lights! Camera! Action! That's how a day begins on a movie set. Behind the scenes you'll find actors busy at work. You'll also see the director and a film crew. Sometimes you'll spot an animal on the set, like Sammy.

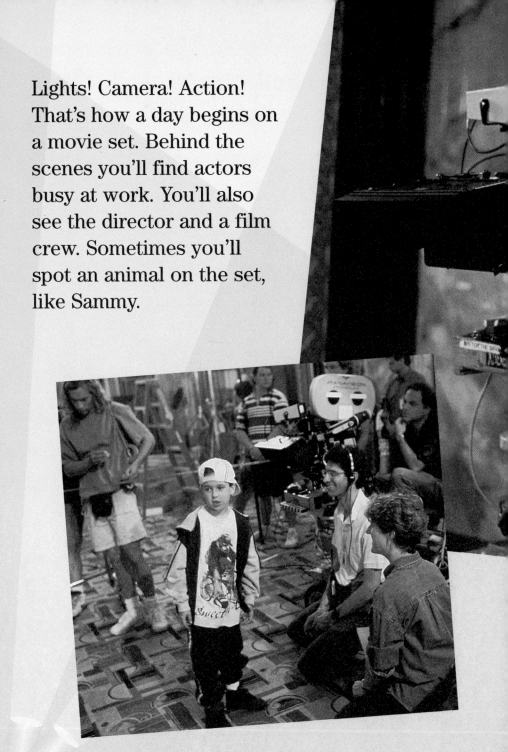

This is Sammy, a six-year-old orangutan. He is one of the actors in the 20th Century Fox movie *Dunston Checks In*. This is Sammy's first movie. It's about a hotel manager who lives with his two sons in a very expensive hotel. One day, a hotel guest brings in a very large trunk. Inside the trunk is Dunston, a young orangutan.

In the story, Dunston sneaks things away from the other hotel guests. The movie follows the funny and exciting adventures Dunston has with the two sons in the hotel.

This is Sammy's trainer, Larry. When Larry was asked to find an orangutan for the movie, he had to find one that could work and play well with people.

As soon as Larry met Sammy, the orangutan hugged him and wrestled with him. Larry could see that Sammy wasn't afraid of people. That's when he knew Sammy was perfect for the part.

Sammy's owners told Larry that Sammy learned quickly and could already follow simple commands to sit and stay. For the movie, Sammy would have to learn how to follow many hand and voice commands from Larry.

Eight months before the movie began, Larry started to train Sammy. He needed to train Sammy to work with lots of different people without fooling around.

Sammy also needed to learn how to wear costumes. In many scenes, he dressed like a robber, wearing a black hat, a black sweater, and black shorts. It was hard for Sammy to keep these clothes on!

Larry worked every day with Sammy to train him how to act and do stunts, like climbing up poles and pieces of furniture on command. Larry was very patient. He knew that Sammy would learn all the tricks needed for the part of Dunston.

At first, Sammy just watched and listened to Larry's commands. Then slowly he learned to do what he was told. Each time he did something right, Larry praised him and gave him a treat. Larry even gave Sammy the nickname, "Mr. Sam I Am." At last he was ready to make a movie!

8

On his first day on the set, Sammy met lots of people. There were people with cameras, the director, and the producer. Everyone thought Sammy was cute and funny. They loved to give Sammy a squeeze. They tried not to laugh when Sammy fooled around on the set. But it was hard not to laugh or make a silly face when Sammy made silly faces.

Soon it was time for Sammy's first scene to be shot. The director told everyone what to do. The cameraman filmed Sammy at work with the other actors.

Sammy really liked Eric, who plays the hotel manager's younger son. Sammy and Eric worked together almost every day. First, Eric had to learn how to act with an orangutan. Sammy also had to learn to follow and listen to Eric. Sometimes it was hard to act out a scene with an ape.

But Eric and Sammy learned quickly and became good friends.

For many days, the whole crew filmed some scenes in a big hotel. In one scene, Sammy and Eric had to sneak out of the hotel room without anyone seeing them.

Sammy had to dress up like an old man. Larry gave him the command to climb into a wheelchair and sit still. Then Eric pushed him out of the room.

Eric and Sammy had to film this scene several times because Sammy kept trying to take off his costume. But he finally did the scene perfectly.

In another scene, Sammy had to
jump into a great big cake. He hung
from a large light and waited for
Larry's signal. Then he jumped.
Sammy was covered with frosting
from head to toe!

There were lots of times in the movie when
Sammy had to swing and climb on things.
These are things that all apes like to do.

In one of the scenes, Sammy had to climb out a window. Larry needed to stay out of sight when he gave Sammy the command to climb. Climbing out was easy for Sammy, but learning how to hang onto the pole and stay still was something new!

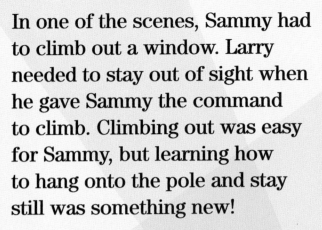

Sammy listened and watched for Larry's command to come down. Soon he heard Larry's whistle and slid down the pole. Then he waited at the bottom of the pole for Larry to give him the command to walk away.

Larry was always behind the scenes helping Sammy perform. He needed to place himself in a spot where Sammy could see and hear him. But he also needed to make sure he wasn't in the way of the film crew. Sometimes Larry found himself in funny positions.

To help Sammy find a picture, Larry had to lie on the floor. Then Larry used hand commands to make Sammy look down at the photograph.

Sometimes Larry did a stunt first and then asked Sammy to do the same thing. It was like the game follow-the-leader. Sammy enjoyed playing this game with Larry.

19

It wasn't all work on the set. There were many breaks. Sammy knew this was the time to have a snack, drink some juice, and relax. Larry's back was the perfect place to rest during break time.

Throughout the entire movie, Sammy stayed close to Larry. He had to be ready when the director needed him to act in a scene.

Soon the movie was over and it was time for Sammy to say good-bye to everyone. He shook hands with Eric. It will be awhile before Sammy and Larry see each other again, too. Sammy helped to make this movie special and everyone will miss him. They can't wait to see Sammy on the BIG screen.

Now that the filming is over, it's time for Sammy to get some sleep. He's learned that acting in front of a camera and being a big star is a lot of fun. But now he also knows that most of the hard work on a movie really happens behind the scenes!

Photo Credits:
All photos courtesy of Twentieth Century Fox Film Corporation

CelebrationPress
ScottForesman
1900 East Lake Avenue
Glenview, IL 60025

ISBN: 0-673-75759-5
LITTLE CELEBRATIONS ® is a registered trademark
of Addison-Wesley Educational Publishers, Inc.,
U.S. Reg. No. 1,765,260.
Printed in the United States of America.

2345678910-BW-0100999897

CelebrationPress

An Imprint of ScottForesman

ISBN 0-673-75759-5

90000

9 780673 757593